How to cope with my loved one's suicide

Janet Haines
Mandy Matthewson

Acknowledgements:
Steven Haines
Robyn Cartledge
Coverart designed by Freepik
(www.freepik.com)

This workbook offers suggestions on how to cope with the death of a loved one from suicide. We do not guarantee that these suggested strategies will resolve all psychological symptoms. You may wish to seek alternative assistance from a mental health professional.

How to cope with my loved one's suicide
Janet Haines & Mandy Matthewson
Copyright © 2025
ISBN: 978-1-923573-18-5

About the authors

Dr Janet Haines has a PhD in Clinical Psychology and has worked as an academic and researcher for 17 years, and in private practice for 30 years helping people facing life problems.

Dr Mandy Matthewson is a Clinical Psychologist, educator and researcher with more than two decades of experience supporting people through life's toughest challenges.

For J.
Strength in the face of heartbreak.

Table of contents

Table of contents 5
Introduction 7
Understanding suicide and suicide risk 8
Impulsivity and planning 12
Challenges from their perspective 13
    Helplessness and hopelessness 13
    Suicidal ideation and changes in thinking 13
    The case of impulsive suicide 13
Challenges from your perspective 14
    Guilt and regret 14
    The search for a reason 15
    The torment of 'what ifs' 16
    Shame and the reaction of others 17
    Feelings of anger 18
    Feelings of relief 18
    The effects on your family 19
Could I have prevented it? 21
    Could I have said something that would have made a difference? 21
    Why didn't they call me? 21
    Was their life so bad? 22
How can I cope with what has happened? 23
Normalising your reaction 24
    Major stressful life events 24
    The notion of a life crisis 25
Allow yourself to grieve 29
    What is grief? 29
    Stages of grief 33
    Tasks of mourning 35
    How long will you experience this grief? 36
    Is grief from suicide different from grief related to other deaths? 36
    Dealing with confusing feelings 36
Manage your emotional reactions 38
    Primary and secondary emotions 38

- Recognising and dealing with your emotions 40
- The link between emotions and behaviour 44
- Learn acceptance 48
  - A change of attitude 48
- Find ways to cope 51
  - Coping 51
  - Problem-focused coping vs. emotion-focused coping 51
  - Problem-approach vs. problem-avoidance coping 52
  - Identifying your preferred coping style 55
  - Building your coping repertoire 58
- Dealing with the demands of others 67
- Some final points 72
- Additional reading 74

Introduction

This workbook aims to help you cope with the death of a loved one by suicide. Every death by suicide is a tragedy. This is true, even in those cases where the reasons for suicide seem to make sense to you. In those cases, the reasons still reflect an intolerable situation for the person who was contemplating ending their life.

The death of a loved one by suicide can present complex challenges for you. Not only do you have to deal with the grief you feel, but you also have to deal with the confusion your loved one's decision has caused you, along with feelings of responsibility or regret that you did not have an opportunity to help that person deal with their problems.

We hope this booklet will help you understand these challenges and deal with this loss in a way that will ease your suffering. We will give you some information about suicide, and then we will provide you with some suggestions about what you can do to help yourself feel less distressed.

Understanding suicide and suicide risk

Suicide refers to the deliberate taking of one's own life. A non-fatal attempt at suicide refers to where the intention was to end life, but, either by choice or circumstance, death does not occur. Parasuicide refers to a behaviour that mimics suicidal behaviour but is carried out for reasons other than ending life (e.g., manipulating someone to change their behaviour). In this workbook, we are focusing on dealing with suicide as a cause of death.

There are multitudes of reasons why people decide to end their life. Each person experiences a cluster of factors that influence their decision. However, some suicides can share features with other suicides. Consider these four groups of suicides:

> A person may suicide after a long history of psychiatric disturbance. There is often a history of suicide attempts and talk of suicide.

> A person may suicide because of depression. There are often feelings of helplessness (nothing they can do to feel better) and hopelessness (nothing will ever change).

> A person may suicide as an impulsive reaction to a stressful life event. Here, something happens, the person becomes distressed and then suicides because they cannot immediately see a way out.

> A person may suicide for seemingly 'rational' reasons. That is, a person may choose to end their life because they are facing a lifetime of pain and ill health that is intolerable for them.

Although these are not comprehensive accounts of why people suicide, they do give you a framework for understanding the suicide of your loved one. It also shows that there is no one reason why people choose to end their life. Further, there may be some overlap. For example, a person may be experiencing chronic pain and be depressed.

A further issue needs to be mentioned. It can be the case that a depressed individual will suicide after it seems that their mood symptoms are improving. This happens because the individual gains the energy and focus to carry through with their intention to end their life when their mood improves but is not yet improved sufficiently to change their perspective about the need to suicide.

As you can see, an understanding of why people choose to end their lives is difficult to achieve because of the many reasons that influence such a decision. The same is true for understanding suicide risk. However, we believe it is necessary to consider the risk of suicide because you are probably thinking about how you should have known that this is what was likely to happen to your loved one. By examining suicide risk, you should be able to see how the assessment of suicide risk is complex.

In assessing suicide risk, a professional undertaking such a task needs to consider the factors listed below. However, it should be noted that a person may experience one or many of these factors and not be suicidal.

Situational factors

    A recent interpersonal crisis (e.g., an argument with a loved one or a relationship breakdown)

    Impending legal issues (i.e., being charged with a crime)

    Financial difficulties

    Imprisonment

    A felt need for revenge

    Intense, angry feelings

    Isolation from others

    Employment problems

    The state of the world

    Loss of a meaningful relationship

    Death of a loved one

Personal factors

    The sex of the person (males are more likely to suicide)

    Age (the risk factors for various age groups vary)

    Living in a rural location (i.e., a place where limited help options are available)

    Personal expectation and self-worthiness (i.e., believing oneself to be not good enough)

    History of mental illness

    History of abuse in childhood

    Drug or alcohol dependency

    Physical illness

    Family history of suicide

    Family history of mental illness

    Body image disturbance

    Unemployment or low socioeconomic status

    Lack of social support or an unwillingness to accept available support

    Membership of a minority group

- Impulsivity (i.e., a tendency to act without adequately thinking through the consequences)
- Perceived inability to cope

There is also a need to take into account imminent warning signs when determining suicide risk. These include the following:

- Sudden changes in the way the person usually interacts with others
  - Either withdrawing from others or not wanting to be around others
  - Withdrawing from physical contact
  - Loss of interest in usual social activities
  - More aggressive behaviour than usual
  - Either loss of humour or acting out like a 'clown.'
- Marked personal changes
  - Decline in work or school performance/disinterest in career
  - Apathy about appearance and dress
  - Lack of concentration
  - Changes in sleep pattern
  - Delusions or hallucinations
  - Sudden happiness after a long period of depression
- Impulsive and risk-taking behaviour
  - Increased alcohol and substance use
  - Careless, accident-prone behaviour
  - Running away, truancy problems
- Making final arrangements
  - Making a will
  - Giving away prized possessions
  - Organising one's own funeral
  - Saying goodbye to important people in their life
- Suicide-related factors
  - History of suicidal behaviour
  - Expression of suicidal thoughts
  - A well-defined suicide plan

Thinking style

>Constricted/black-and-white thinking (e.g., "either be miserable forever or suicide")

>Hopelessness about the future

>Errors in thinking (e.g., predicting catastrophe)

No single one of these factors will identify suicide risk. However, a combination of these factors is taken into account by helping professionals who are determining the suicide risk of any individual. What should be evident from this list is just how difficult and complex a task it is to identify when someone is at risk of suicide. It is a difficult task for professional people who are trained in suicide risk assessment to identify successfully the people at imminent risk of suicide. How can you expect to have been able to do this? It is asking too much of yourself to suppose you should have known what would happen.

Let's consider some factors that warrant further attention to help you understand what happened.

Impulsivity and planning

The death of your loved one may have come as a complete shock to you or may have been the thing you have been dreading the most, knowing that your loved one has been talking about suicide for some time. This is the case for a number of reasons.

Firstly, some people who suicide have talked about it, and some people never talk about it. There are some myths about this very fact. For example, some people believe that if a person talks about suicide, they will not do it. Of course, this is not the case. In reality, although some people who suicide never mention their intentions to anyone, others talk about their suicidal thoughts. Some will mention it occasionally, and others will talk about suicide continually.

This can be explained partially by our second point. Some suicides are planned out, whereas others occur impulsively. Some people will develop a plan for how they will do it and consider it for a period of time. For others, there is no extended period of premeditation. Something will happen, and they will decide, then and there, to end their lives.

It is worth mentioning that other people talk about suicide but never follow through and act on their suicidal thoughts. The point we want to make here is that even if a person talks about suicide, it does not follow that you could have done anything to prevent it. We will talk about this more in a moment.

Before moving on, there is one important point that should be raised when discussing impulsivity and suicide. There is a link between alcohol intoxication and suicide. This is because alcohol intoxication can remove the usual constraints a person may have on their decision-making and actions. When sober, a person can think more clearly about the consequences of their choices. When intoxicated, people are more likely to act impulsively.

Challenges from their perspective

There are a number of factors that relate to the suicidal person that you need to consider when attempting to understand why your loved one decided to end their life.

Helplessness and hopelessness

People who have been struggling to cope well over a period of time can start to feel both helpless and hopeless. Helplessness refers to a belief that there is nothing they could do to fix their problem. This may be caused by repeated, unsuccessful attempts to solve their problem situation or it may result from a period when they did not even try because they believed the problem was too overwhelming.

Feelings of hopelessness develop. This is the belief that nothing will ever change. It feels like there is no sense in trying to make things better if nothing will ever improve.

This combined feeling of helplessness and hopelessness can be overwhelming. People can then start to think about suicide as the only way forward.

Suicidal ideation and changes in thinking

As a person starts to think about suicide, the nature of their thinking changes. Feeling helpless and hopeless, they see things in black-and-white terms. That is, they come to believe that they will either have to suffer forever or they will have to end their life. This is referred to as constricted thinking because the ability to think in a flexible way to solve a problem is limited. Further, the more they think about suicide, the more acceptable it seems. It is hard to pull their thinking away from this rigid view.

The case of impulsive suicide

Of course, this longer-term thinking about suicide is not evident in people who impulsively decide to end their life. In these cases, the problem they face feels overwhelming, and they cannot see anything other than poor outcomes. Suicide then seems like a viable option for that person.

The size of the problem they are facing is not the fact that will determine if suicide is considered. The problem that triggers this decision may seem quite solvable to other people. It is how overwhelming that problem seems to the individual rather than the objective size of the problem that will lead to suicidal thinking.

Challenges from your perspective

The challenges for you we are referring to here come after the suicide of your loved one, although your thoughts may take you back to times before your loved one died. In all likelihood, you will feel overwhelmed by thoughts that you could have or should have done something more than what you realistically could have done to prevent this from happening.

Guilt and regret

In the aftermath of the death of a loved one to suicide, you will likely experience strong and difficult emotions. These feelings are over and above the feelings of grief and loss that would be expected from the death of someone important to you.

You may feel regret, believing you could have or should have done something more than you did to try to prevent the suicide. This feeling can be strong, and it is that strength of feeling that causes you to believe what you are thinking. That is, you believe that it must be true because you are feeling something strongly.

The trouble with this view is that there are errors in this way of thinking. To start, it is a mistake to assume that because you feel something strongly, it must be true. That feeling is not the thing that will determine objective truth. Indeed, feelings are subjective rather than being objective indicators of fact.

There is an important point to be made here. What this means in terms of the strength of your reaction to the suicide of a loved one is that you need to look elsewhere to determine whether these bad feelings are justified, not just listen to your internal voice that is telling you that you should have done something.

There is a second error in thinking that you should have done something more to prevent the suicide from happening. The error here is thinking there was an identifiable thing you could have done that would have made a difference. If there were such a thing to be done, people would do it, and then, far fewer people would die by suicide than is the case. However, there are a few problems here. Firstly, even if you intervened at one point in time, such as visiting your loved one at a dark moment in their lives, it does not mean that your loved one would not choose to take their life at some other point in time. You could not permanently be available to prevent something from happening, no matter how much you wanted to be able to help.

Secondly, even if you had an opportunity to intervene, it would be difficult to know what you should have done. The motivations for suicide and the individual issues that contribute to a person's decision to suicide are complex. To know what to do is to ask a lot of yourself when even trained professionals cannot guarantee that an intervention of any particular type will ensure that suicide will not occur.

Thirdly, a belief that there was something you could have done would need to be based on the knowledge that the suicide was going to occur and when it was going to happen. Of course, in most cases, you do not know these things about your loved one. Even in those cases when your loved one had spoken about suicide, you could not have known for sure when the intervention was needed.

Despite all of this, you may experience intense feelings of guilt about the suicide of your loved one. This guilty feeling can be triggered by a range of thoughts you might have about what has happened. For example, you may go over in your mind the last few times you spoke and what you might have said or not said at those times. You might worry about how long it has been since you contacted your loved one and what implication that might have had on the decision to suicide by your loved one.

In this way, you may feel responsibility for what happened—however, this feeling of responsibility is not your burden. No matter what came before, the decision to suicide was made by your loved one. If there were a strong and direct link between problematic interactions with the people you love and suicide, there would be a much higher suicide rate, and people would be too scared to even disagree with someone they cared about.

> *Prior to his best friend's death by suicide, Marcus was well and truly fed up with his friend's miserable mood. Although he knew the low mood wasn't his friend's fault, he started feeling annoyed by his constant negativity and grim outlook about everything. Nevertheless, Marcus tried to be patient and supported his friend as best as possible. After his friend died by suicide, Marcus felt overwhelmed by feelings of guilt. Even though Marcus had never told anyone he had felt fed up, and even though his friend never knew how he was feeling, Marcus hated himself for failing his friend. These guilty feelings led Marcus to believe that there was something he could have done that he had failed to do.*

The search for a reason

You can torment yourself searching for a reason why your loved one chose to end their life. You can feel that there should be an explanation that will make sense to you. However, this is unlikely to be found. To fully understand their decision, you would have to be able to put yourself in their shoes at the moment they made the decision and in the time after that moment. Of course, no matter how close you were to your loved one or how much you understood their points of view in general, it is not easy to fully understand what a person was thinking and how they were reacting to the things that were happening to them at a time when their thinking was not clear.

> *Ben couldn't stop thinking about his daughter's decision to end her life. Nothing about it seemed to make any sense to him. He spoke with family members and his daughter's friends and colleagues from her place of work. Although he gathered some information about what was going on in his daughter's life, about which he had been previously unaware, nothing seemed to be the sort of thing that he thought would cause his daughter to take her own life. So, Ben kept searching for an explanation that would satisfy him. He wanted a reason to allow him to understand and have peace of mind.*

The torment of 'what ifs'

You will likely be inundated with thoughts about how the outcome could have been different 'if only'. The list of possible 'if only' or 'what if' events could be endless.

> If only I had visited or phoned.
>
> If only they had told me how they were feeling.
>
> If only too many things had not happened all at once.
>
> If only their relationship had worked out better.
>
> If only they had gone to the doctor earlier.
>
> If only they had sought some help.

You will generate a long list of things that might have made a difference, but they did not because those things did not happen. In all likelihood, none of these things could be guaranteed to have changed the outcome. Even if they had temporarily changed the course of events, what happened in the longer term may have remained the same.

In any case, the outcome cannot be changed because none of those things you are tormenting yourself with actually happened. In fact, the suicide occurred because of a chain of events that came before. That chain might have been a long one, with lots of complicated events contributing to it, or a short one in that it occurred in the hours or days before the suicide. In both cases, that chain of events has already happened, and no amount of wishful thinking will change that.

The challenge for you is to accept this. You can learn to accept that this happened because of all the other events that had already happened and that nothing can alter that fact. By accepting what has happened, you are encouraged to focus on coping with the present and look to the future rather than torment yourself with a past you wish had happened differently but did not happen. We will talk more about acceptance later.

> *Jennifer kept going through her mind all the things that led up to her husband taking his own life. She knew he had been struggling at work and worried about money. Over time, he got more and more depressed. Jennifer thought she should have insisted he seek help when she suggested it to him. She felt that things might have turned out differently if she had only made it clear to him how much he meant to her and that she didn't care about a bigger house and a new car. She thought about how things might have turned out differently had she come home earlier that day instead of going to the supermarket on the way home from work. She wondered what would have happened if she had thought to phone him that afternoon. These thoughts went around and around in her head. If only...*

Shame and the reaction of others

At a time when you most need support, you may feel unable to seek the support you need. It can feel more difficult to say a loved one has died by suicide than for another reason.

The difficulties you face in disclosing what has happened may be related to your fear of how people will react and how that reaction might differ from the response you could get from people if your loved one had died of another cause. You may be concerned that people will be judgmental and form ill-informed opinions about you and your loved ones. You may feel that you would receive less genuine sympathy than you would get if the cause of death of your loved one had been anything other than suicide. You might fear potential gossip if people start to learn of what happened.

You may wish to avoid telling other people what has happened because talking about it invites a discussion you do not want to have at that time. Sometimes, it is difficult to deal with other people's reactions to the suicide of your loved one and their questions about what happened when you have not yet dealt with your own reaction to your loss.

Although it may be important for you to receive the support you need, to obtain this support, you may feel a need to provide explanations. It is possible for you to discuss your grief and loss without disclosing the fact that a loved one suicided. After all, whether or not you tell someone is up to you. Things that happen to you are your private business, and you should be the one who decides what you disclose. Remember that a person's curiosity does not obligate you to provide personal and private information. There is no problem with discussing suicide, but only if you choose to do so. We will discuss ways to manage people's curiosity later in the workbook.

> *Carolyn was dealing with her sister's death by suicide. Her sister had battled drug dependence problems for a long time and all of the issues in life that drug use brings. And now she was gone. Carolyn had told her employer that she was unwell but hadn't disclosed her sister had died. She knew that if her colleagues learned of her sister's death, they would ask questions about how she had died. If they learned she had died by suicide, they would ask questions about why. The thought of having to answer these questions or dodge answering them was more than she could bear. She hadn't told these people about her sister's problems before and didn't want to tell them now. She just didn't know how they would react. She was afraid they would judge her sister. Carolyn was worried they would respond to her differently if they learned her sister had died.*

Feelings of anger

The loss of a loved one can trigger angry feelings. This can be confusing when these angry feelings conflict with feelings of love and loss. However, the angry feelings become understandable when consideration is given to the source of the anger. In many cases, following the death of a loved one by any cause, a person can experience feelings of abandonment and rejection, as if they have been left to cope with life without the person they love. This is especially true when the person who died has deliberately chosen to end their life and, therefore, abandon their loved one.

The challenge is to recognise that these angry feelings are a normal part of the grieving process for many people. They do not detract from the depth of feeling you have for the person who has died. Indeed, it could be argued that they are a reflection of that feeling. The anger comes from experiencing the loss and not because of negative feelings towards the person you have lost, even though that may be how the emotions are expressed.

> *Angela's husband had taken his own life. As much as she did not want this to happen, she had not been surprised that he had done this. She had worried for a long time that this would happen and had done all she could to help him. What surprised her was how angry she felt. She was furious that he had left her to deal with all their financial troubles and that he had deprived her of the future they had planned together. But, mostly, she was angry that he had deprived their two young children of their father and had left her to deal with their loss. Angela hid her anger from everyone as best she could. She thought they would never understand why she was feeling so angry.*

Feelings of relief

The feelings of loss you experience can be complicated by feelings of relief. This can occur in cases when a suicidal person has had a long history of psychiatric problems and difficult behaviour with repeated suicide attempts. This experience can cause family members and loved ones to exist in a permanent state of crisis and apprehension, not knowing what will happen next. After the death of the loved one, the sense of relief can be overwhelming. This person can then view themselves as bad for feeling this way. However, given the turmoil they have been through, it is not unreasonable to feel relief that the turmoil has ended. Being relieved that the turmoil has ended is not the same as being glad someone is dead.

A feeling of relief might also be experienced when a person with a debilitating physical or psychiatric condition ends their life. In this case, the relief may come because that person is no longer suffering pain and ill health. It is difficult to watch a loved one suffer when there is nothing you can do to alleviate that suffering.

This sense of relief should not diminish other feelings of grief. In all likelihood, the time will come when these other feelings will take priority, and the sense of relief will be pushed to the back of your mind. Remember, the relief you are feeling is most probably related to the end of the anxiety and distress you have been experiencing over an extended period of time.

> *Olivia told everyone she was heartbroken that her sister had ended her own life. She was heartbroken. However, she also felt a sense of relief that overwhelmed her other feelings about her sister and what happened. For a long time... years... Olivia had been affected by the chaos of her sister's life that she understood to be caused by her sister's mental health problems. It seemed her sister had lurched from one crisis to the next, and Olivia always had to swoop in and fix things for her. Whenever her sister was faced with a problem she had created for herself, she called Olivia. Financial difficulties, legal problems, alcohol abuse, drug use, terrible relationships, evictions from rented properties, accidents and injuries, it was always Olivia who would come to the rescue. She had willingly provided a home for her niece and nephew to give them stability. But Olivia had been worn down by her sister's life situation. She had reached a point where she was exhausted and anxious, always expecting the next crisis to happen. So, secretly, Olivia was glad all the chaos and crises had stopped. The tears she shed were, at least in part, tears of relief.*

The effects on your family

A suicide in the family can bring the members of the family closer together. However, it can also tear a family apart. There can be accusations of wrongdoing and attributions of blame. At a time of intense distress, opinions are formed that may not be made at times when family members are calmer and thinking more clearly.

The best thing you can do is recognise the distress everyone is feeling and choose to step back from the interactions characterised by blame and animosity. You do not have to involve yourself in other people's reactions. Instead, you should focus on how you are feeling and how you should cope with those feelings. This does not mean that you cannot or should not support family members. It does mean that you do not have to be drawn into the complicated range of emotions other people are experiencing. Give yourself time to reflect on what has happened and make sense of this experience.

> *Jack's brother, the youngest of four siblings, had taken his own life while in a drunken state. Jack was trying hard to understand what had happened and why, both in terms of his brother's decision to suicide and what had happened to his family as a consequence. His mother, who Jack had to admit had never been a very effective parent, seemed to be making it all about her, carrying on to her group of friends that no one could appreciate her trauma and demanding to know why her son had done this to her. His father was rarely around, and no one seemed to know where he was going or what he was doing. Jack's oldest sister was angrily demanding why none of her family members had known that her little brother was at risk of suicide, accusing other family of doing too little to help him. His other sister wouldn't get out of bed. Jack felt like he was standing in the middle of a storm.*

In reflecting on what has happened, you are likely to ask yourself difficult questions about the death of your loved one and the decision they made to end their life.

Could I have prevented it?

The truthful answer is no, you could not have prevented it. If someone is determined to take their own life, there is very little you can do. You could have encouraged them to talk. You could have encouraged them to seek professional help. However, they may have chosen to simply disregard your suggestions. You could have followed them around, sat with them, or observed them. But there would have come a time when they were unattended and that might have been the moment when they followed through with their plans. So, if someone is determined to take their own life, they will do so whether or not you act to prevent it. It is that determination that will be related to the outcome, not whether or not you could have acted in a way to try to prevent it from happening.

Could I have said something that would have made a difference?

You may torment yourself, believing that if you just had the right words and were given the opportunity, you could have talked your loved one out of taking their own life. In reality, there are no right words that would have guaranteed that your loved one would have changed their mind. Remember, people who are suicidal have a change in their thinking. They make errors in thinking such that they would not necessarily have seen the rationality of what you were saying to them. You could have made all the sense in the world, and your suicidal loved one simply may not have been able to agree with you.

> *Robert had a small group of close friends who had been best mates since their school days. Recently, one member of the group had taken his own life after the breakdown of his marriage. This had been a huge shock to them all, and the loss of their friend had been a source of great distress. Robert couldn't get it out of his head that he could have said something that would have convinced his friend not to do this. He kept playing over in his mind the things he might have said... if he had had the chance. So sure was he that he could have said the right thing that would have made a difference to the outcome that he felt strong and overwhelming waves of regret that he did not have the opportunity. Going over in his mind what he wanted to have had the chance to say to his friend was having a negative effect on Robert. He couldn't sleep at night, and he couldn't concentrate at work during the day. His friends tried to reassure him that there was nothing he could have said that would have made a difference, but Robert didn't believe this. There must have been something that would have made a difference.*

Why didn't they call me?

Undoubtedly, you would have helped if they had reached out to you and you felt there was genuine cause for concern. However, it is often the case that people who are considering suicide will either not reach out or not tell you of the seriousness of their thoughts if they do. Indeed, a failure to reach out can be an indication of their intention to end their life.

> *Leah didn't understand why her friend, Noah, had not let her know that he was thinking about ending his life. She kept thinking about the last time they had caught up for a coffee, trying to remember if there was any indication that something was wrong. She analysed everything she remembered him saying that might have given her a clue about what was about to happen. But, mostly, Leah was questioning what sort of friend she truly was if Noah had not reached out to her when he needed her the most. She thought they were close, so she couldn't understand why Noah hadn't reached out to her for help.*

Was their life so bad?

It can be confusing for you to examine the circumstances of your loved one's life to try to understand why they took their own life. You have to remember that it is not whether or not their life was objectively bad, it was how they perceived it to be.

There are many reasons why people die by suicide. It is hard for anyone to understand those reasons when the person trying to understand is not in the same state of mind as the suicidal person. Your thinking is clearer and not affected by errors and distortions that are apparent for suicidal individuals. You would have been able to see ways to resolve problems they would not have been able to see. Even if you gave them a more rational interpretation of their situation, they may have rejected it.

> *Eric's 19-year-old son died by suicide. Eric struggled to understand why this had happened. From what Eric could learn, his son had the same ups and downs as other young people his age. That his son would take his own life didn't make sense to Eric. He had his whole future ahead of him, with many opportunities he could have explored. Eric's wife, who was devastated by the death of their son, thought Eric was being unsympathetic. But that wasn't the case. Eric was just confused by his son's decision and couldn't make sense of what he had done.*

So, given that this has happened and you could not have prevented it, how do you learn to cope with what has occurred? Let's consider that next.

How can I cope with what has happened?

In coping with what has happened, it may help to do the following:

To start, it helps to understand that your reactions are a normal response to an intensely stressful event in your life. We will introduce you to the notion of a major stressful life event and why such events present a challenge to the people experiencing them. Then, we will outline the process we go through when we are faced with a crisis in our lives. This will allow you to put your reaction to your loss in the context of how we deal with significantly challenging life experiences.

You should allow yourself to grieve. It is helpful to understand grief and the grieving process so that you can understand that what you are experiencing is not a sign of mental disturbance, no matter how difficult your psychological experiences might be. We will introduce you to the grieving process.

Understanding that your emotional reactions are part of a normal grieving process does not prevent you from choosing to control your emotional reactions so that their intensity does not overwhelm you. Learning to focus on your emotional reaction can prevent you from having to experience a string of additional emotional reactions triggered by your initial feeling and are unnecessary. You can also learn about the link between your emotional state and your choices to behave in particular ways. This can help you feel you have greater control of what you are doing at a time when your emotions can overwhelm you.

With your emotional reactions under greater control, you can learn to accept what has happened as something you cannot change. This will help you focus on what you need in the present and work towards coping well in the future.

If you feel you do not have a way of coping with what has happened, you can learn about ways of coping so that you can take advantage of your coping strengths or develop these strengths.

Finally, you can learn to understand your rights so you can protect yourself during this difficult time. These include your right to privacy, your ability to say no when others make demands on you, and your right to ask for help. We will help you understand and apply these rights.

Normalising your reaction

At a time when you are feeling overwhelmed by your emotions, it is hard to appreciate that your feelings are a normal reaction to a stressful event in your life. Often, when you are feeling intense emotional reactions, it feels like no one else could feel this way or this badly. This is especially the case if you have not experienced an event before that has triggered a similar reaction in you. Let's consider how this experience fits our understanding of stressful life events.

Major stressful life events

First, you probably need to consider what is happening in the context of other life events you may have experienced. The death of a loved one is usually considered a major stressful life event. What does this mean? A major stressful life event is something that happens to a person that causes them to feel distressed, and that has a significant impact on their life and well-being.

Not all events in your life that stress you would be considered major stressful life events. For example, getting a speeding ticket or misplacing your credit card is stressful, but it is not a major stressful life event. These other types of events require that you do something to fix the problem, but they are the sort of difficulties you will get stressed about and then recover from as soon as they are over.

When researchers first started thinking about how events in our lives differ in terms of how distressing they are, they got people to rate various events in terms of how stressful they were considered to be and how much of an impact they had on a person's life. In this way, the most stressful of the major stressful life events were those that were the most stressful *and* had the most significant impact.

When we look at the major life events that cause the greatest stress and have the biggest impact, among the most stressful are:

> Death of a spouse or death of your child
>
> Divorce
>
> Marital/relationship separation
>
> Death of a close family member other than a spouse or your child

So, you can see that the death of a loved one is understood to be one of the most stressful experiences with which a person has to cope, whether or not the death was by suicide.

Due to the severe nature of a major stressful life event, we must expect a difficult time when it occurs. And that is true when a loved one dies. You will be facing a challenging time for a while. You will then adjust to what has happened. This is not to say that you will just move on, but you will adapt to the change in the circumstances of your life.

The notion of a life crisis

This idea that you are in for a difficult time but will reach a point where you will adapt and move forward with your life fits with what we know about how people cope with a life crisis.

So, how do we cope with a life crisis? As we go through life, most of us face challenging times. We have learned how people react to these experiences. Although people are individuals and how we cope with difficult times may differ to some degree, there seems to be an underlying pattern to how we cope with crises in our lives.

We react to the shocking nature of the crisis

When we first learn of these types of events, such as learning of the suicide of your loved one, we tend to go into a shocked state. Although we understand something bad has happened, we tend to feel like the events are unreal. That sense of unreality can be explained.

The pressure placed on us at these times triggers a chemical reaction in our brains that protects us from the enormity of what has happened. Your brain sorts out quickly that you need to do what is necessary to get by, so this chemical process protects you from the full emotional impact in those early stages. The reaction to this chemical process, called dissociation, typically occurs when we experience intense stress. It can be felt as *depersonalisation*. This is where you feel disengaged from what you are doing, and it is experienced in a way that makes you feel like you are observing yourself from a distance. It can also be felt as *derealisation*. This is experienced in the sense that what is happening around you is like a movie being played rather than a real-life experience.

The feeling can be uncomfortable despite the experience of dissociation being helpful, protecting you from the full emotional impact of what you have experienced until you are in a better position to cope. You will feel disengaged from events around you, and it is harder to make sense of things and process complex information about what has occurred and what you need to do. For example, people will tell you things you fail to remember. It is best to understand this state as your brain putting you in survival mode. You will be able to handle what you need to do to get by but feel disengaged and distant from what has happened.

This feeling can last for a short period or for days. Also, you can move in and out of this state as new aspects of your crisis become apparent. With each stressful thing you experience, your brain will put you back in a state that is self-protective but uncomfortable and unpleasant.

> *Yesterday, Eliza learned that her daughter had died by suicide. Her son-in-law had phoned and told Eliza and her husband that he had found his wife when he returned home from work. Her husband had immediately gone to their daughter's home but Eliza hadn't wanted to go. When her husband returned, she saw he was upset, but nothing seemed real. Now Eliza was trying to make sense of the news but felt she was living in a thick fog. She realised her lips felt numb, and she thought that was odd. Other family members had gathered at her home, but Eliza had difficulty understanding what they were saying when they spoke to her. Her husband and other children wanted her opinion about funeral arrangements, but every time she tried to concentrate, her mind would drift off. It wasn't that she was thinking about other things. It was more that she couldn't think about anything. Eliza attempted to comfort her children, but it felt strange doing that. Really, she wished they would just go somewhere else so she could sit quietly.*

The best thing you can do when you are in this state is to not put undue pressure on yourself. When you are in that disengaged, dissociative state, it is not the time to make big decisions or reach conclusions about what you must do from here on. Remember, you are in survival mode and incapable of complex thinking about important matters. Also, know that this state will end, and you will have time to plan and make decisions after this state has ended. Take advantage of this state. Remember that it occurs to protect you from the full emotional impact of the loss of your loved one.

We then go on an emotional roller coaster ride

When we come out of this shocked state, the full impact of the emotional cost of the experience is felt. After a period of feeling disengaged and unsettled, we then feel emotionally overwhelmed and emotionally out of control. It feels like you have no idea how you will feel from moment to moment. Feelings can change from intense sadness and despair to fearfulness about the future, and then to anger. Your emotions will be volatile, and the immediate emotional state you are experiencing will come and go without an objective trigger. A thought will just go through your mind, and your emotional state will change.

This will be a really difficult time for you. The intensity of your feelings will challenge your ability to cope at times. Unfortunately, this emotional roller coaster ride can continue for some time, although the nature of your emotional response may change. You may feel sad, anxious, angry, or panicky. The feelings can be intense and overwhelming.

> *Eliza thought she was probably going crazy. She knew she was grieving, but she just hadn't expected it to feel like this. In a way, it was all right when she cried because that made sense to her. After all, grieving people cried, didn't they? But she didn't know what to make of all the other feelings she was having. Sometimes she was so angry although she wasn't quite sure where her anger was directed... sometimes her daughter, sometimes the world for being so unfair, sometimes her son-in-law although she knew he loved her daughter, sometimes herself for not knowing sooner how much trouble her daughter was experiencing. And, to her shame, she sometimes felt so resentful that she thought her head would explode... resentful because her nice, organised life had been turned upside down by her daughter's decision. She pitied her family and friends who had been trying to support her. She thought they never knew which version of her they would get when they visited or phoned her. Eliza thought she was being silly, but she also became incredibly anxious about the safety of her remaining children. She would call them at work to hear their voices and know they were okay. Eliza had had some ups and downs in her life but never experienced this level of intensity of emotions. She didn't like it, but there didn't seem to be anything she could do to stop it.*

We then enter a period of reflection

The emotional roller coaster ride will end. It will be exhausting and stretch your capacity to cope, but there will come a time when it is over. You will then start to reflect on what has happened and what it means. This period of reflection comes at a time when your emotional state is under control enough for you to think more clearly about what has happened and how you move forward.

This is an integral part of adjusting to what has happened. You have to try to make sense of what has occurred. After coming out the other end of the emotional roller coaster ride, you will be better positioned to think clearly about the important aspects of your experience. You will be better positioned to adjust your views about what has happened and perhaps view it from a different point of view.

> *Over the last few weeks, Eliza had been thinking about her daughter. From early on in her life, Eliza knew her daughter was a sensitive soul who wasn't as resilient as her other children. She had worried about her when she was a child because she would be so easily upset by normal disagreements with her friends. Eliza thought about the times she had tried to ease her daughter's passage through life as she got older. She had been happy when her daughter met and married her husband, thinking that his support would make her life better. But, in the end, she supposed that her daughter just couldn't cope with the normal stressors in life. It made Eliza sad that her daughter couldn't find a way to take pleasure in the things in life that others found so easy to enjoy.*

We then reach a point where we can move forward

There will be people who will tell you that you will 'get over' what has happened. However, that is not what occurs. You will reach a point where you will have integrated your experience into what you know about life and your place in the world. You will become the new version of you who has had this happen to them. In that way, you will become wiser with greater life experience. You may look back at the difficult time with sadness, wishing that things had worked out differently, but you will also be in a position to deal with the reality of the situation and move forward, living the next stage of your life.

In this way, you should avoid trying to fight to get back the old version of you. It is not possible, and it is not necessary. The new version of you can be happy. The new version can look to the future with optimism. These things will be determined by you and not by what has happened to you. It is hard to imagine that might be the case when you are in the middle of the emotional difficulties that come with the death of a loved one, but these things are the case whether or not you currently believe it is possible.

> *Eliza's life had taken on a rhythm that was comforting. She missed her daughter and thought about her every day but not with the same level of emotional pain she had felt before. She had found a way to understand that life was too difficult for her daughter. Eliza thought about ways her daughter had changed her. She was proud to have been her mother. Her daughter also had helped her to be more aware of how others around her were coping. She felt that she was a better person and believed that was her daughter's doing.*

Please be aware that these reactions are normal. That is, the reaction you have is a normal response to a stressful situation, even though these feelings seem so negative and overwhelming.

Allow yourself to grieve

We all think we understand grief… until we experience it. Then, it seems much bigger and more overwhelming than we thought possible. On top of your grief, you are also feeling a complex range of emotions and being burdened by the confusing thoughts related to the death of a loved one by suicide. But let's start to gain a better understanding by clarifying what we mean by a grief reaction and how people experience this.

What is grief?

Grief is a universally experienced emotional reaction to loss or perceived loss. It can also be experienced in relation to expected loss (anticipatory grief). However, most commonly, it is experienced with regard to the loss of someone or something important to you.

Acute grief

Acute grief occurs after the death of a loved one. These feelings of grief occur irrespective of the cause of death. This type of grief is associated with severe or intense feelings of distress.

> *Kayla felt like she couldn't take a deep breath in. She felt like she was going to tip over the edge and fall into a deep abyss. She didn't know how she was going to be able to cope with these feelings. She could not image surviving this emotional onslaught. Kayla's husband had taken his own life, and she was trying to make sense of what had happened. She had never felt this distressed before. It was overwhelming. No one could comfort her. She couldn't bear to be around people, but she couldn't bear to be alone. Even being surrounded by people who cared about her did not ease the intense loneliness. The strength of her emotions made her feel panicked, and then she felt frightened by the panicky feelings. She couldn't see how this feeling would ever end.*

In the initial phases of acute grief, you can feel shock and numbness. You feel disengaged from what is happening. This dissociative experience is protective, in a sense, from the intensity of the emotional reactions. However, there will come a time when the full strength of your emotional reactions will be felt.

The emotional reactions to the loss you have experienced can be varied and may change over the course of the period of acute grief. Examples of the types of grief reactions are identified below.

Table 1: A list of the ways in which people can express their grief.

Shock	Anguish
Loss	Anger
Guilt	Regret
Anxiety	Fear
Intrusive images	Depersonalisation
Feeling overwhelmed	Loneliness
Sadness	Depression
Longing	Emptiness

Let's consider an example.

> *David always considered himself to be a pretty down-to-earth sort of person. He rarely got upset about things. He used to laugh and shake his head when people around him would become stressed over things he considered not worth his energy. He had assumed he would always be this way and would always be able to cope. Then, his brother took his own life. David was hit with a confusing array of emotions he couldn't recall ever experiencing. He had never realised he could experience such emotional turmoil. One minute he was overwhelmed by sadness and feelings of longing for his brother to come back to him. Then he was angry with his brother. Then he was frightened that these feelings would never go away. Then, the sadness would return in such a profound way that he didn't know how he would be able to cope with it.*

These emotional reactions have been described as the most painful feelings an individual can experience. In the beginning, they may seem to be always present. However, before long, this changes, and you experience grief in bursts or waves. These waves of grief tend to be triggered by reminders of what has happened or things that make you think of the person you have lost.

> *David would think for a moment that he was feeling better. However, he would then be hit with a wave of emotion so strong that it would take his breath away. This wave of grief would occur when there were obvious reminders of his brother and what had happened. Even the mention of his brother's name would be enough to trigger this overwhelming burst of distress. But it was also triggered by indirect reminders. When he got into his car, he was hit by a wave of distress because he remembered the last time he had been in the car with his brother. The unexpected nature of these reminders made it difficult for David. He felt he couldn't predict how he was going to be feeling from one moment to the next. He felt that nothing was stable anymore.*

These waves of grief lessen over time, both in their frequency of occurrence and their strength or intensity. This reduction will allow you to regain a feeling of emotional balance. At this time, your attention will be more focused on events outside of you than your emotional state.

> *Although there were times when the breath was knocked out of David by the waves of grief he felt, he realised that these waves were not coming as frequently or lasting as long. He found himself being distracted by things, such as work. In fact, it was a relief to be back at work because it allowed him to feel almost like his normal self for periods of time. He realised he would feel distressed again when he stopped concentrating on other things. So, David liked to keep himself busy as much as he could.*

Integrated grief

Integrated grief is experienced after you transition beyond the acute grief stage. To reach a point of integrated grief may take you several months or more or may occur sooner.

There are signs of you having reached integrated grief. For example, you can think about the person you have lost without the overwhelming nature of your earlier emotional responses. You can pick up your life again, returning to work and engaging in activities that give you pleasure.

> *Although he still strongly felt the loss of his brother, David found he could do more of the things he would normally do to keep him busy. He was able to concentrate better at work. He started to meet up with friends and engage in social activities with them. Sometimes, he felt like he was in a strange place between upset and distressed and his more usual down-to-earth way of looking at the world. He wasn't quite sure where he should be between these two states, but he felt he was moving in the right direction.*

It is often the case that you can move forward with a better perspective on life, a greater understanding of what is important in life, and a new focus on the things that matter. These positive changes in outlook have been identified to occur after a serious and often traumatic life event. That life event acts as a catalyst for you to change your outlook on life. It causes you to reprioritise things so that you focus more on the important issues in your life and less on the more minor things that no longer matter.

> *Although never a person to get upset about minor hassles, David recognised that he was guilty of sometimes neglecting his important relationships when he was busy with his life. After the death of his brother, and now that he was feeling a bit better, David was taking the time to keep in touch with his sister and to spend more time with his parents. It seemed like a natural thing to do. In fact, he thought it wasn't even a conscious decision to treat his family better. Instead, it was something he wanted to do, so spending more time with his family was no hardship.*

For most people, there is a point where you move on with your life, being the new person you have become due to the loss you have experienced. However, this is more challenging to achieve for a small number of people.

Complicated grief

As stated, for a small number of people, there will be a struggle to overcome their acute grief. This prolonged acute grief reaction is known as complicated grief, among other things. The feelings of longing and loss do not decrease over time. For these people, it is difficult to re-establish their lives in any meaningful way without the person they have lost.

Indicators of complicated grief include ongoing waves of grief that do not diminish in intensity and a combination of preoccupation with the person who has died mixed with strong avoidance of reminders of the loss they have experienced. The person may become focused on death. They are unable to reach a point where they can experience happy memories of their loved one. These people become stuck in their loss and misery.

> *Cynthia's son had died by suicide over two years ago. It was the most devastating thing that she had ever experienced. Other members of Cynthia's family had come to terms with what happened and had dealt with their grief in various ways. But Cynthia didn't seem able to do this. She felt as bad today about the loss of her son as she had when she learned of his death. She couldn't bring herself to engage in any pleasurable activities that others thought might make her feel better. She didn't want to. To enjoy herself felt like a betrayal of her son. She cried every day. She couldn't talk to others about her son because that would make her feel even more distressed, and she didn't want to talk to them about anything else. As time passed, she became increasingly isolated. She had withdrawn from her husband, her other children and her friends. She didn't think it was possible to ever recover from what had happened.*

Complicated grief is not the typical outcome of a grieving process. Most people transition through to a point where they can experience life in a meaningful way.

Stages of grief

When we discuss the experience of grief, we often talk about it in terms of the stages of grieving people go through to reach a point of readjustment. In its simplest form, five stages of grief have been described.

Denial

The denial stage is triggered by learning of the death of a loved one. It allows you to take a step back from the enormity of what has happened because you cannot yet absorb the full impact of what has occurred. It is a protective stage in that sense. It allows you to slow down the rate at which you process this emotionally painful experience. As you feel more able to deal with the reality of the loss, you will leave this stage.

Anger

The denial stage is typically followed by a period when you experience angry feelings. You can feel angry towards the person who has died because they have left you. This can be especially true in cases of suicide when the decision made by the loved one to end their life can feel like an abandonment of you. However, in the absence of the loved one, you can find that you direct your anger towards others, who may be undeserving, and even towards yourself. However, as you begin to process the loss you have experienced, your anger will end.

Bargaining

Feelings of anger are replaced with a process of bargaining. In effect, you are bargaining for a better outcome than the one you are experiencing. For example, you might bargain for the return of your loved one, promising to do things better if this had just not occurred. Alternatively, you might bargain for the removal of the pain you are experiencing, again promising to be a better person if you are allowed to feel less overwhelmed and upset.

This can be a difficult process. You live in a world of 'if only' and 'what if'. You go back over painful things and promise to do them better if given a second chance. This can lead to you blaming yourself for things beyond your control. Even though you are trying to negotiate yourself out of a situation that seems intolerable, you do not have the ability to achieve your goal.

Depression

As a result of you realising there is nothing you can do to change your situation, your mood can drop to a low level. You can become profoundly sad and feel empty and lonely. Although this is a normal reaction to great loss and is one that will end, you develop a feeling that you will never recover. You may withdraw from activities that would normally be interesting to you, and you can pull back from people who would normally support you.

As stated, this is a normal reaction to the loss you have experienced. It is part of a healing process and a move towards recovery rather than a sign of mental illness. However, you may interpret your strong reaction as a sign of mental ill health. This can be worrying for you as this interpretation of your feelings can lead you to believe that you are experiencing a permanent state from which you will not recover.

Acceptance

The final stage is one of acceptance. This occurs as you recover from the feelings of depression. You start to feel more able to deal with normal life challenges and engage in normal life activities.

However, it is incorrect to assume that you will 'get over' what has happened or return to your 'old self'. Indeed, you will become a new version of yourself. You will be the person who has now experienced this great loss. You will readjust to life without your loved one, so you will not be an identical version of yourself that existed before the loss. This is normal and expected. It is impossible to go through life and be unaffected by our experiences, especially our profound experiences.

This stage can also be a difficult one. As you move to readjustment following a loss, you can experience emotional reactions that are confusing and challenging. For example, it is a common experience to feel guilty when you catch yourself enjoying an activity or experiencing a period of time when you have not thought about your lost loved one. It is not the case that you should feel guilty as you have done nothing wrong. Please see these feelings as a sign you are readjusting, not a sign of wrongdoing.

These five stages of grief are commonly described. Other, more complex accounts of the stages of grief exist. It is interesting to note that whether you consider your experience in the context of a life crisis or as a grieving process with various stages, there are considerable similarities in these conceptualisations.

Tasks of mourning

Another way of looking at the process of dealing with the death of a loved one by suicide is to focus on what is required of you rather than seeing it as a more passive experience of these stages. A psychologist named J. William Worden described what he saw as the four tasks of mourning. Instead of viewing it as a progression through stages, he considered that people will move back and forward between these tasks as they deal with their grief. The four tasks of mourning are as follows.

Task 1: Accept that the loss is real

It can be difficult to accept the reality of the loss you have experienced. On the one hand, you can intellectually know that your loved one has died, but on the other hand, it is a difficult emotional concept to grasp. As a result, you experience feelings of disbelief, even though you know it is true that your loved one has died.

The acceptance of the reality of the death of your loved one can create a challenge for you. Although you may be faced with the reality of what has happened early on, the harsh realities can fade. You can then be hit with the reality again at some other point in time, perhaps when there is a reminder of the enormity of your loss.

Task 2: Process the pain of grief

The pain associated with grief can be all-encompassing. It affects you emotionally, intellectually, physically and, for many people, spiritually or philosophically. Many people will expect that you will 'get over' your grief. However, to process the pain of grief, it may be necessary to express your feelings and describe your experiences to process the pain that grief triggers.

Task 3: Adjust to a world without the person who died

In adjusting to living in a world without the person who has died, you are faced with multiple ways this adjustment must occur. There are external adjustments in that you might have to take on new roles or demonstrate newly learned skills to fill gaps left by your loved one. There are internal adjustments that you have to come to terms with now being a person who has experienced this loss. It would be best if you considered how this experience might have changed your view of yourself and how you fit into the world. Adjustments may be made regarding your spiritual or philosophical view of the world because your previous belief system has been challenged.

Task 4: Find a way to have an ongoing connection with the person who died while moving forward with a new life

You need to find a way to reach a balance between your ongoing connection with the person who has died and going on to live a life of good quality and a life with purpose.

These tasks of mourning are normal and, for most people, will be completed at some point. However, finding ways to assist in these adjustments may be advantageous. Whether or not you find ways to help yourself with these tasks, they will be undertaken as a normal response to grief.

How long will you experience this grief?

There is research that suggests that acute grief reactions start to decrease after about six months. However, it can take some people up to two years for this to occur. Although this can seem overwhelming, and you might question your capacity to cope with such a long period of grief, you need to remember that your reaction to what has happened does not stay at that intense phase throughout this period. Your reactions change as you go through a period of adjustment. In this way, your feelings will not be as overwhelming as they are at their peak, and the pain you feel will not be consistently intense.

Is grief from suicide different from grief related to other deaths?

Whether a grief reaction to the death of a loved one from suicide is the same as the death of a loved one from some other cause cannot be answered in a straightforward way. This difficulty relates to how researchers gather and analyse information rather than being particularly confusing.

What we can say is that most of the differences between the way people grieve following the death of a loved one to suicide when compared with how people react to other deaths disappear when a particular comparison is made. That is, the differences disappear when the grief from the death of a loved one to suicide is compared with the grief experienced by people who are grieving the loss of a loved one from an unexpected and/or violent cause. It seems that the differences relate more to how prepared you are for the death of your loved one than to suicide itself.

Dealing with confusing feelings

It is important that you understand that you are facing a confusing array of emotions, some of which will relate to the grief you feel about the death of your loved one and some which will relate to the choice they made to end their own life. You need to allow yourself to grieve, irrespective of how you feel about the fact that they ended their life by suicide.

Manage your emotional reactions

Before we move on to learning how to improve and take advantage of your coping skills, it is worthwhile to spend some time learning about ways to control your emotional reactions to stressful events. This will help you accept your situation, allowing you to feel more settled and less distressed. It will also help you reduce the intensity of the emotions you feel in reaction to the loss of your loved one.

Primary and secondary emotions

Emotions are your reactions to the things that happen to you or the things you think about. When something good happens, you will feel pleasurable emotions and respond positively to your situation. You will experience distressing emotions when something bad happens and you view your situation negatively.

Human beings can experience a full range of emotional responses, from strongly negative to strongly positive. We are complex creatures with the capacity to experience a range of emotions due to any one event. Sometimes, this can be overwhelming. It then makes sense to be able to regulate your emotions so that your emotional state does not overwhelm you.

Let's consider how we react emotionally. When something happens, we experience an emotional response. These initial responses are referred to as primary emotions. They are our reactions to our experiences.

However, as we are complex individuals, we can then develop an emotional reaction to our initial emotional reaction. These emotions are referred to as *secondary emotions.* Secondary emotions refer to the feelings we have about our feelings. Let's consider an example. You go to the cinema with a friend to see a movie. The movie's content makes you feel sad, and you burst into tears. Then, afterwards, you feel embarrassed that you felt so sad and cried in front of your friend. The sadness you felt about the movie was your primary emotion. It was your initial reaction to what was happening. The embarrassment you felt was your secondary emotion. This was the feeling you had in response to your primary emotion.

Our secondary emotions can become quite complex. Consider the following example.

Example of complex emotions	
What happened?	*I have to sort out and pack up the possessions of my loved one who died.*
How do you feel?	*I feel anxious* (primary emotion).
How do you react to the anxiety?	*I don't like feeling anxious, and I want that feeling to go away.*
What do you say to yourself?	*"This is going to be terrible."* *"I wish I didn't have to do it."* *"What if I can't cope?"* *"This will just remind me of what had happened."*
What do you feel now?	*I feel sad* (secondary emotion).
How do you react to the sadness?	*I don't like the feeling, and I want it to go away.*
What do you say to yourself?	*"Now I just feel overwhelmed by sadness."* *"I shouldn't have to feel this way."* *"If only they hadn't made this decision to end their life."*
What do you feel now?	*I feel angry* (secondary emotion).
How do you react to this feeling?	*I feel uncomfortable and stressed.*
What do you say to yourself?	*"I shouldn't feel angry at them when they are not here to defend themselves."*
What do you feel now?	*I feel guilty* (secondary emotion).

So, instead of just feeling anxious, you now feel anxious, sad, angry and guilty. Your primary emotion is anxiety, and all the rest are secondary emotions.

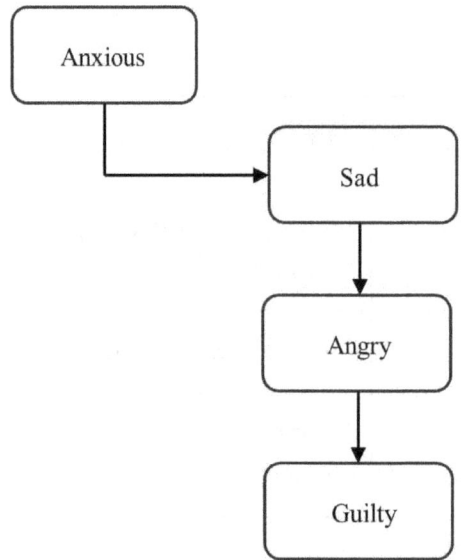

Figure 1: Diagram of primary emotion leading to secondary emotions.

One way to stop this process is to focus your attention and coping efforts on your presenting emotional state. For example, if you feel anxious, give this emotion your attention and work on coping with it. The anxiety you are feeling is your primary emotion at that time. It is the emotion you feel directly because of what you are facing.

Your emotional reactions can be difficult to manage because what started as a straightforward emotional response to a stressful event turns into a confusing array of emotions. Sometimes, these emotions can compete with each other and pull you in different directions. For example, you can feel both sad and angry, or angry and excited. Trying to deal with one of these emotions can be undermined by your efforts to deal with the other emotion.

Recognising and dealing with your emotions

When dealing with difficult situations, simplifying things is necessary. You can learn to focus on your primary emotions as they arise and adopt strategies to deal with them. Let's start by looking at a way to identify your emotions so you know what to give your attention to.

> *What happened?*
>
>> Here, consider the situation that developed, resulting in you feeling these strong emotions.
>
> *Why did this situation occur?*
>
>> Consider the possible causes of the problem situation. This is an important step. It gives you the opportunity to interpret the situation's meaning in an

> effort to help you understand why you are feeling the strong emotions you are experiencing.

How were you feeling as a result of that situation?

> Identify your primary emotional response to the situation and then consider the secondary emotions you experience.

What is it that you wanted to do as a result of how you were feeling?

> Here, we refer to the urges or impulses you have to act in response to your emotional state. When feeling strong emotions, people tend to experience urges to take more extreme actions.

> It does not follow that the person will always do these things; however, thoughts about doing them can be present. It is worth noting that people tend to think about doing extreme things much more often than they ever do them. This means that you control the impulse to act in an 'over-the-top' way. If you can control these impulses, you can control others in a way that will allow you to have a more settled and reasonable response to provoking situations.

What did you actually do and say?

> Here, you are considering what you actually did rather than what you had an urge to do.

After experiencing those emotions and actions, how did they affect you?

> Here, we are referring to the consequences of experiencing those strong emotional states and your reactions to those states when you choose to act in a particular way.

Let's start by taking the process of experiencing an emotional reaction a step at a time. Let's consider the job you are undertaking to sort through and pack up your loved one's possessions.

Understanding your emotions worksheet - example
Time and date: *Thursday, 10th.*
What happened? *I have to go through all their things and decide what to keep and what to get rid of.*
Why did this situation occur? *There are two reasons why I am in this situation. Firstly, this has to be done because my brother ended his life. Secondly, I am the person who offered to do this because I couldn't let my mother be the person who had to do it.*
How were you feeling as a result of that situation? *I feel really anxious about going there* (primary emotion) *and looking through his things. The fact that I am anxious about it makes me feel really sad* (secondary emotion) *because he was my brother, and I should be able to do this for him. The fact that I then have to feel sad just makes me angry* (secondary emotion). *This is all his fault because he suicided. But I have no right to feel angry, and it just makes me feel guilty when I get angry at him* (secondary emotion).
What is it that you wanted to do as a result of how you were feeling? *I wanted to go to bed and hide. I thought it would be easier if I just burned down his house.*
What did you actually do and say? *I just reminded myself that there was nothing to feel anxious about. I took a deep breath and reminded myself that this is something important I can do for my brother. I also phoned my cousin and asked if they would help me, and they were happy to do that for me.*
After experiencing those emotions and actions, how did they affect you? *Initially, I felt overwhelmed and exhausted before I even started clearing out his things. But after I dealt with my anxiety and asked my cousin for help, I felt more settled and more able to do the task. I still wasn't looking forward to it, but at least I thought I could cope without falling apart.*

We suggest you use the worksheet below to try to understand what you are feeling and why you are feeling it. It is designed to help you understand how you are reacting to the problems you are facing, which may direct you to how you can cope with the situation.

Understanding your emotions worksheet
Time and date:
What happened?
Why did this situation occur?
How were you feeling as a result of that situation?
What is it that you wanted to do as a result of how you were feeling?
What did you actually do and say?
After experiencing those emotions and actions, how did they affect you?

Worksheet available at elemen.com.au

Remember, your goal here is to focus on your primary emotion. If you can resolve your primary reaction to the problem you are facing, other secondary emotions may either not occur or simply resolve. When you experience secondary emotions, tell yourself that you will focus your energy on your primary emotional reaction. You can then give your attention to finding ways to cope with the triggering source of your distress.

The link between emotions and behaviour

When you are faced with situations outside your control, you can feel strong emotions. This can be a difficult and uncomfortable time. It would be helpful for you to be able to manage those strong emotions.

This does not mean that you should fight against the emotions you feel. You cannot start a war with your emotional state and expect to be the victor. However, you cannot ignore your emotions and expect them just to disappear. The aim should be to recognise and validate your emotional reactions but do what you can to avoid escalating emotional distress.

Understanding the link between your emotional state and the things you choose to do in response to that emotion is worthwhile. It is difficult to control your behaviour choices if you do not appreciate the link between how you feel and what you do.

Let's consider how you might behave in relation to your emotional responses. Consider this example.

Imagine that you have experienced an argument with family members about the funeral arrangements for your loved one. They wanted a private funeral with only the closest family members present. You felt that your loved one's friends should be able to attend and participate in a demonstration of how much your loved one meant to people.	
I felt	What I did
Angry	*I became increasingly upset and told my family that if they were going to be stubborn, I wouldn't attend the funeral. Then I stormed out of the room and went home. I refused to answer their calls.*

Understanding this link between your emotional state and your behaviour can help you learn to make different choices when you are upset. Let's consider how you might opt to do things differently. Consider the same example, but now let's look at how this person might have chosen to behave in an alternative way.

I felt…	What I did	What I could have done instead
Angry	*I became increasingly upset and told my family that if they were going to be stubborn, I wouldn't attend the funeral. Then I stormed out of the room and went home. I refused to answer their calls.*	*I could have explored with them their reasons for wanting a private funeral. I could have reminded them that he was much more than his final decision to end his life and that he had many friends who were important to him. However, if they were insistent about a private funeral, I could have arranged a separate get-together for his friends at some time after the funeral.*

Let's take this one step further and consider the likely outcomes of the initial behaviour choice and the alternative one.

I felt	*Angry*
I did…	*I became increasingly upset and told my family that if they were going to be stubborn, I wouldn't attend the funeral. Then I stormed out of the room and went home. I refused to answer their calls.*
What happened?	*I continued to feel angry and upset. My family became unhappy with me and blamed me for making a challenging time even more difficult. I ended up going to the funeral but didn't talk to my family members. I ended up being more upset than I needed to be.*
A better choice…	*I could have explored with them their reasons for wanting a private funeral. I could have reminded them that he was much more than his final decision to end his life and that he had many friends who were important to him. If they were really insistent on having a private funeral, I could have arranged a separate get-together for his friends.*
Likely outcome…	*I would have been disappointed about the private funeral, but I could have attended with my family there to support me. His friends would have understood and would have been happy to attend a separate get-together, where I could have been surrounded by people who would have shared stories about my brother that would have made me happy.*

Initially, you can work on thinking up alternative and healthier behaviours after the event. This will allow you to learn how to make better choices by considering the different outcomes of various behaviours. It will then become easier to apply this strategy when you are feeling the emotional reaction so that you can choose better behaviour and avoid doing things that might feel all right at the time but do not help you in the long term. Below is a worksheet you can use.

The emotion-behaviour link worksheet
I feel/felt…
I did/I felt the urge to do…
What happened/what would have happened?
A better choice…
Likely outcome…

Worksheet available at elemen.com.au

You will feel better if your emotional state is more under your control. This does not protect you from strong emotions, but it does allow you to handle them in manageable ways. It can help you reach a point where you have accepted what has happened, and this will allow you to adjust.

Learn acceptance

To cope with overwhelming emotional states, such as those that can develop when you must deal with the loss of a loved one to suicide, it is necessary to learn ways to manage the distress you feel.

A change of attitude

Typically, when stressful events occur, we react to them in the context of something being done to us or happening to us. If we hold someone else responsible, we tend to react with anger and resentment, believing that the person involved should have done something other than what they did. If we hold ourselves responsible, we tend to focus on self-criticism and regret. The result is that we start a battle within ourselves about the event. The more we focus on our anger and resentment, or our self-criticism and regret, the more distressed we tend to feel about our experiences that triggered these feelings.

The trouble with this approach is that it does not really let us accept and deal with the fact that the event has actually happened and that we must cope with it… because we have little choice. We focus more on the past, which we cannot change, and give less attention to the present and the future, over which we can exert some control.

> *Brayden's cousin died by suicide. Growing up, they had been very close… like brothers. This closeness continued throughout their teen years. However, their lives took different directions as they entered adulthood, and they spent less time together. It got to the point where they rarely saw each other. Brayden was unaware that his cousin was experiencing problems. After his cousin's death, Brayden couldn't stop thinking about how things might have been different if he and his cousin had remained close. He kept thinking that he would have been aware of what was going on in his cousin's life and would have fixed things for him. Brayden felt certain he could have helped his cousin if only he had been aware of what was happening. Brayden was angry with his cousin for not letting him know what was going on, and he was angry with himself for having drifted apart from his cousin. He thought he could not forgive himself for not being there for his cousin.*

When you are dealing with the death of a loved one to suicide, you are faced with ongoing challenges. Most of these challenges are not things you would choose to have to face. This can cause you to experience distress when and even after the challenges occur.

To cope with this, you need to consider changing your attitude to one of acceptance rather than being tormented by events that you cannot change. Many things can happen that cause you pain and emotional upset. The more you focus on these situations, the more distress you tend to feel. The goal here is to learn to accept things you cannot change.

Often, when we have to deal with a challenge we did not want, we get upset, thinking that this should not have happened or should not have happened to us. Rather than battle events that have already occurred in this way, the goal is to accept that they *did* happen and that it is now appropriate for you to deal with these changed situations.

Being distressed about a situation does not help you cope with that situation. It is a fact that you cannot change the past. Nevertheless, we tend to emotionally react to these situations as if there is something we can do to change them. In doing this, you become stuck and do not look for other, more effective ways of coping with your new circumstance.

In learning acceptance, you need to acknowledge your changed situation without trying to control it or change things that have already happened. Try to understand that your current situation has occurred because a long chain of events in the past brought you to this point. Your job now is to use your coping skills to move forward with life, as it is a waste of your energy and effort to torment yourself thinking "if only…" or "what if…".

This type of acceptance does not mean you cannot wish things had turned out differently. It also does not stop you from looking for ways to manage or improve your current situation or avoid things that might happen in the future. This type of acceptance asks you to look at your situation and accept it for what it is. From here, you can choose what you want to do about it.

Whenever you feel overwhelmed by your situation, you can use simple coping statements reminding you that a position of acceptance is preferable. Consider the following coping statements. Add anything you can think of that would help you accept what has happened so that you can move forward and deal with things as they arise.

Acceptance coping statements	
Below are some examples of coping statements that may help you achieve acceptance. These coping statements remind you to accept your situation and the events that contributed to your current situation. Tick the coping statements you may find useful, and then add any others you believe will help. Then, when you feel overwhelmed, use these coping statements to help you manage your reaction to the events that are stressing you.	
	Things are the way they are.
	There is a chain of things that contributed to what is happening now.
	I cannot change things that have already happened.
	There is no point battling past events.
	Battling the past upsets my present.

	I can only deal with the present.
	It is a waste of my energy to try to change the past.
	The present is as it should be, even if it is not my choice.
	This moment in time has occurred because of all the things that came before.
Add your own coping statements	

Checklist available at elemen.com.au

By adopting the view you cannot change what has already occurred, you are then able to focus your attention and effort on coping with the present and preparing for the future.

Find ways to cope

We are going to examine ways you can cope. We will explore the fact that people have preferred coping styles, and your best chance of coping well is to build up your coping strategies in the way that best suits you. Let's start to explore coping in general and your preferred coping style.

Coping

We all have our own coping resources and individual coping skills. When we refer to coping resources, we are talking about the things we have available to help us cope. Coping skills refer to the strategies we use to deal with the problems we experience. We all have our own particular coping resources and specific coping skills because there is not one particular way of coping.

In a general sense, the way you will cope with the problems you are facing about the death of your loved one will likely be a reflection of the way you have dealt with and solved other problems throughout your life. That is, the way you cope will reflect your general style of coping.

Your goal should be to understand how you cope and to make good use of the coping resources you have or can create, as well as the particular skills you have developed or can develop. This is true even if you take into account the fact that dealing with the loss of a loved one to suicide may be a more challenging problem than other problems you have dealt with in your life. For those of you who feel you do not cope well with life problems, it may be the case you have been trying to develop coping skills based on a pattern of coping that does not suit you.

To understand the way you cope and to use this knowledge to choose the best strategies to cope with the death of your loved one, consideration needs to be given to the fundamental differences people can have in the way they approach problem situations. Let's consider the different approaches to coping so that you can work out your preferred coping style.

Problem-focused coping vs. emotion-focused coping

To start, a distinction can be made between problem-focused coping strategies and emotion-focused strategies.

Who are problem-focused copers?

Problem-focused copers deal with their problems by considering the problem situation and trying to fix it. They tend to want to *do* something when confronted with a problem. They are most comfortable when there are specific things related to the problem that can be the focus of their attention. In the context of the suicide of a loved one, problem-focused copers are the ones who will look for ways to actively engage in activities that would allow them to feel in more emotional control, such as seeking out information about suicide or organising the funeral.

Who are emotion-focused copers?

Emotion-focused copers are the people who deal with their problems by expressing their emotional reactions to the situation. They will talk about the problem and cry when they feel the need. They see the value of sharing their feelings about their problem to others. In the context of the suicide of your loved one, the emotion-focused coper will cry and talk to a friend about how they are feeling.

Are people either emotion-focused or problem-focused copers?

Some people are strongly problem-focused copers, and some people are strongly emotion-focused copers. Others fall somewhere on the continuum between the two extreme positions. You may be more problem-focused than emotion-focused but still use some emotion-focused strategies… or the reverse.

If you already have a good idea of where on the continuum you fall, you can do a little exercise to find your coping preferences or confirm them. But first, we have to consider one other element.

Problem-approach vs. problem-avoidance coping

People assume that when we talk about coping strategies, we refer to good ones that will help us deal with our problems. This is not the case. People's coping styles can be divided by whether they tend to confront their problems or whether they prefer to avoid them. This is the case for both problem-focused and emotion-focused copers.

Let's start by looking at problem-focused coping. How would problem approach and problem avoidance strategies differ. Consider the examples in the table below.

Table 2: Examples of problem-focused approach and avoidance strategies.

Problem-focused, problem approach strategies	Problem-focused, problem avoidance strategies

Problem solving
 	
Problem solving coping strategies involve:
 	
    Examining the problem
 	
    Generating potential solutions
 	
    Evaluating the likelihood of a successful outcome
 	
    Moving forward and applying the strategy
	Problem avoidance
	
	Problem avoidance coping strategies involve:
	
	    Deliberately avoiding thinking about the problem
	
	    Deliberately avoiding reminders of the problem

Cognitive restructuring
 	
Cognitive restructuring coping strategies involve:
 	
    Reframing your thoughts to think more reasonably about the problem
 	
    Correcting errors in thinking that are barriers to coping with the problem
	Wishful thinking
	
	Wishful thinking as a coping strategy involves:
	
	    Wishing the problem would go away
	
	    Indulging in thoughts that things will return to 'normal'
	
	    Spending time thinking about how things will work out in your favour and as you wish

With regard to the suicide of your loved one, the effective, problem-focused approach coping strategies may help in the following ways. They may help you generate ideas of how to solve specific problems you face, such as wrapping up your loved one's affairs. They may also help you to work out ways that you can cope more effectively with the demands being placed on you, such as deciding on ways that could help you deal with challenges that develop, for example, arranging a funeral or having a plan of what to do if you feel emotionally overwhelmed.

Now let's consider emotion-focused coping. The table below details examples of approach and avoidance emotion-focused coping strategies.

Table 3: Examples of emotion-focused approach and avoidance strategies.

Emotion-focused, problem approach strategies	Emotion-focused, problem avoidance strategies
Emotion expression Emotion expression as a coping strategy involves: Being open and talking about how you are feeling Allowing yourself to experience your emotional reactions in relation to the problem Using emotional expression as a form of catharsis, letting off steam to allow yourself to feel better for a while	*Self-criticism* Self-criticism as a coping strategy involves: Blaming yourself for the problem Criticising yourself for failing to control your emotional reaction to the problem Viewing yourself as more generally deficient than is warranted
Social support Using social support as a coping strategy involves: Turning to family and friends for support Talking with your support network about how you are feeling Taking comfort from your support people Allowing your support network to offer instrumental/practical support	*Social withdrawal* Social withdrawal as a copy strategy involves: Cutting yourself off from family and friends Failing to seek professional support when it is needed Refusing assistance offered by the people who wish to help you or would be willing to do so

When we consider the suicide of your loved one, the effective emotion-focused approach coping strategies may be of assistance to you in the following ways. They may allow you to express your emotional reactions and deal with them rather than bottle them up. They may result in you choosing to seek support from your family and friends or from a grief counsellor to allow you to discuss how you are feeling and, potentially, resolve some of those feelings that can be overwhelming if they are kept hidden.

Identifying your preferred coping style

The goal here is to identify the type of coping that works best for you. If you are an emotion-focused coper, you may see the value of a problem-focused coping strategy but it is unlikely that you could comfortably be able to adopt problem-focused coping strategies and expect them to work for you. Your efforts would be better directed at taking advantage of your preferred style of coping and use problem-approach strategies that best suit you.

Here is an exercise in determining what type of coping style best characterises your preferred type. Tick the boxes if you typically use the listed coping strategy to deal with problems you face.

	How do I normally cope?
Problem solving	
	I work on finding ways to solve the problems I face.
	I work out what I should do, and then I follow the plan.
	I like to work out a plan and then move forward.
	I believe there is a solution to every problem.
Problem avoidance	
	I try to act like nothing is wrong.
	When faced with a problem, I choose not to do anything, even when I know I should.
	I try not to spend any time thinking about the problem.
	When the problem comes to mind, I push it out of my head.
Cognitive restructuring	
	I think about my problems in a way that allows me to realise I can manage them.
	I think about the problem to change the way I react to it.
	I try to look on the bright side of any situation.

	I try to put things into perspective.
Wishful thinking	
	When faced with a problem, I just wish it would go away.
	I just hope a miracle will happen to make everything all right.
	I hope the problem will fix itself.
	I wish that someone would come and fix the problem for me.
Emotion expression	
	When faced with a problem, I allow myself to express my feelings about it.
	I do not try to bottle up my feelings; I let them go so that I can feel better.
	I do not hide my feelings about the problem from other people.
	When faced with a problem, I just need some time to experience my feelings.
Self-criticism	
	I blame myself for the problem I am facing.
	I ask myself what I have done to make the problem happen.
	I tend to hold myself responsible for the problems I face.
	When a problem occurs, I feel I should have done things differently.
Social support	
	I turn to the people I know will listen when I talk about how I feel.
	I feel better when I can talk to others about my problems.
	When faced with a problem, I seek advice from people I trust.
	I allow other people to offer help and support when I am dealing with a problem.

	Social withdrawal
	When faced with a problem, I like to avoid other people and spend time by myself.
	When I am struggling with a problem, I do not want to be around other people.
	I do not share my thoughts and feelings with others.
	I do not accept the help others offer.

Checklist available at elemen.com.au

What type of coper are you? Add up the ticks you placed in each category and enter the number in the following table.

Ways of coping score sheet	
Problem-focused strategies	*Emotion-focused strategies*
____ Problem-solving ____ Cognitive restructuring ____ Problem avoidance ____ Wishful thinking ____ **Total**	____ Emotion expression ____ Social support ____ Self-criticism ____ Social withdrawal ____ **Total**
Problem-approach strategies	*Problem-avoidance strategies*
____ Problem-solving ____ Cognitive restructuring ____ Emotion expression ____ Social support ____ **Total**	____ Problem-avoidance ____ Wishful thinking ____ Self-criticism ____ Social withdrawal ____ **Total**

Score sheet available at elemen.com.au

When comparing your problem-focused and emotion-focused strategies, see where you have scored the highest. This may show a strong preference for one type of coping strategy or the other. If so, you can build on your preferred coping type when considering what coping strategies will help you with your current situation. If you have similar totals for both problem-focused and emotion-focused strategies, you would do best to include each type in your coping plan.

When considering whether you use problem-approach strategies or problem-avoidance strategies, you are considering whether adjustments must be made in how you cope. If you predominantly use problem-avoidance strategies, you can learn to abandon those in favour of problem-approach strategies while staying within the same style of coping strategy, that is, problem-focused or emotion-focused.

Building your coping repertoire

Now that you better understand how you cope, you can start to build a plan for moving forward, adopting coping strategies that work for you. Let's consider some examples of coping strategies you could adopt.

Problem-focused strategies

We will start by looking at problem-solving strategies. Here, you are trying to devise a plan for solving a specific problem situation, followed by decision-making regarding which potential solution you would choose. You then should be able to follow through and try to solve your problem.

Let's consider an example of this process.

Example of a problem-solving strategy
What is the problem? Clearly define the problem you are facing. *I have taken on most of the arrangements and paperwork that need to be done because my family members are too upset to cope with them. I now feel overwhelmed by how much I have to do.*

Generate as many possible solutions as you can. List the ones that are likely to work.
 	
I could do the following:
 	
    I could just stop complaining and get on with things.
 	
    I could tell other family members they have to help me.
 	
    I could prioritise the importance of the things I have to do and focus only on the most urgent ones.

Consider the likelihood of each of these strategies being successful. *Although I could just get on with things, it doesn't seem likely that this would work. I am already feeling overwhelmed, and if I keep doing what I have been doing, this will not improve. I would likely reach a point where I cannot continue, and then nothing will get done.* *I could get family members to assist me, but I am not sure how much help they would be given how they are reacting to the loss of our loved one. Also, I'm unsure how I would feel about forcing them to do something that I believe would exceed their capacity to cope.* *If I prioritise the importance of the things I have to do, I can then undertake the tasks in a more orderly way and get a sense of what needs to be done as soon as possible.*
Select the problem-solving strategy that is likely to work the best. *I choose to prioritise everything I have to do. If I do this, I should be able to avoid feeling overwhelmed by the 'big picture'. Not everything is as urgent as everything else. There are some timeframes that I can take into account. Wanting everything done at once is not the same as <u>needing</u> everything done at once.*
What are you going to do next? *I will make a list of everything I have to do. Then, I will consider these things in terms of their urgency (i.e., when they need to be done) and work out a timetable that will not overwhelm me and allow me some time to think about my own emotional state.*

In this example, the person has considered the problem and identified possible options for resolving it. The person then considers the likely outcome for each potential solution. They choose their preferred solution and devise a plan for their next step. This is a good problem-solving approach.

Here is a problem-solving worksheet you can use.

Problem-solving strategy worksheet
What is the problem? Clearly define the problem you are facing.
Generate as many possible solutions as you can. List the ones that are likely to work.
Consider the likelihood of each of these strategies being successful.
Select the problem-solving strategy that is likely to work the best.
What am I going to do next?

Worksheet available at elemen.com.au

Let us now consider a cognitive restructuring approach to coping. Below is an example of a cognitive restructuring approach to addressing a problem situation.

Example of a cognitive restructuring strategy
What is the problem? *I didn't phone my brother for three weeks before his death.*
What are you thinking? *I should have phoned. I might have been able to prevent his death if I had phoned him.*
What evidence do you have that this is true? *It is true that I didn't phone him, but I can't think of any evidence that what I am thinking is true.*
What evidence do you have against this being true? *I had gone for three weeks or more before without phoning him, and he had gone for even longer without phoning me, and everything was ok. Even if I had phoned, I would only have known that something was wrong if he had told me and he had spoken with other family members in those three weeks without mentioning that he intended to take his own life.*
Even if it was true, what is the worst thing that would happen? *Even if it was true that I should have phoned, the fact is that I didn't, and this was not particularly unusual. Believing that I might have been able to help if I phoned is not the same thing as actually being able to help. I would have had to be psychic to know what he intended to do if he didn't tell me or anyone else there was a problem.*
What do you conclude? *It is unlikely that my phoning him would have made a difference. Other family members had phoned him, and they couldn't stop what happened because he didn't tell us there was a problem. It might have made me feel better if I had phoned him, but I suppose I would have found something else to be concerned about, such as asking myself why he didn't tell me there was a problem when I phoned. I have to conclude that I am just trying to make sense of what happened rather than blaming myself for something I didn't know about. My sister made good sense when she said, "You can't know what you don't know".*

Here, the person in this example challenged the way they were thinking about their situation. They then examined whether the situation was a realistic point of view. Having realised that was not the case, they then worked out a better, more realistic way of thinking about their problem. You can see that their alternative thoughts about their situation would make it easier for them to cope. They would not be tormented by thoughts that they had not done enough. Instead, they could be more accepting of their situation and realise that they could not have changed anything, as much as they would have liked to have done so.

Below is a worksheet you can use to consider a cognitive restructuring coping strategy.

Cognitive restructuring strategy worksheet
What is the problem?
What am I thinking?
What evidence do I have that this is true?
What evidence do I have against this being true?
Even if it was true, what is the worst thing that would happen?
What is my conclusion?

Worksheet available at elemen.com.au

Emotion-focused strategies

Next, we will consider how to enhance your emotional expression coping skills.

Example of an emotion expression strategy
What is the problem? *I learned that my brother died and that he had taken his own life.*
What did you do? *I tried to be strong and be there for my mother in case she needed me to do something.*
What were the advantages of doing this? *I don't really know. I didn't really help Mum or myself.*
What were the disadvantages of doing this? *I felt like my head was going to explode. I felt like I was going to fall apart. I worried that no one would hold everything together if I fell apart. People knew I was holding it together for Mum and were worried about me when they should have just been focused on dealing with their own feelings.*
What could I have done differently? *I could have expressed how I was really feeling about the news. I could have allowed myself to cry and be upset.*
What would the advantages have been of doing things this other way? *I would have felt some relief. I wouldn't have felt like my head was about to explode, and I would have got rid of the knot in my stomach. I think I could have helped others more, including Mum, if I had just taken the chance to share how I was feeling.*
Would there have been any disadvantage of doing things this other way? *Not that I can think of. Most of my family members knew I was only pretending to be okay. They worried about me at a time when they should have been focusing on how they were feeling.*
What will you do next time you feel like this? *Next time I feel like that, I will be honest about my emotions and express them in a way that lets me react better and genuinely be okay instead of pretending to be OK.*

In this case, the person went through a process of examining the pros and cons of both not expressing their emotions and expressing their emotions in response to the news they received. The conclusion was reached that the better option was to allow themselves to react in a genuine way to what they were feeling.

Below is a worksheet you can use to develop emotion expression coping strategies.

Emotion expression strategy worksheet
What is the problem?
What did I do?
What were the advantages of doing this?
What were the disadvantages of doing this?
What could I have done differently?
What would the advantages have been of doing things this other way?
Would there have been any disadvantages of doing things this other way?

What will I do next time I feel like this?

Worksheet available at elemen.com.au

Finally, we can consider how to use social support as a coping strategy.

Example of social support as a strategy
What is the problem? *I was overwhelmed by the news that my brother had ended his life and felt I couldn't cope.*
What have you done in response to this problem? *I tried to hold everything together for Mum, but when she didn't really need me to do that, I went home and hid.*
How has responding in this way helped you with your problem? *Well, it hasn't, really. I felt distant from everyone and didn't have a clue how I was going to cope with the news. I felt as overwhelmed and unable to cope as I did before I went home and hid.*
What could you do instead? *I could have turned to my family for support, and I would have felt less lonely in our shared grief. I could have reached out to my friends, who I know would have offered me support and good advice. They would have looked after me at a time when I really needed someone to lean on.*
How would this be likely to work out? *My family would have shared their feelings with me and supported me the best way they could. I know my friends would have rallied around me and offered me support and advice. I would have felt better and not so overwhelmed.*
So, what are you going to do next? *I will increase my contact with my friends during this difficult time and spend time with my family members.*

Here, the person thought through their situation and realised they were doing the opposite of what they should have been doing to fix their problem of feeling overwhelmed and unable to cope. They realised the solution was available to them and that pursuing it had advantages. It was then easy to follow through with their plan and reach out to others.

Below is a worksheet for you to use with a social support coping strategy.

Social support strategy worksheet
What is the problem?
What have I done in response to this problem?
How has responding in this way helped me with my problem?
What could I do instead?
How would this be likely to work out?
So, what am I going to do next?

Worksheet available at elemen.com.au

In moving forward, remember to choose the coping strategy that best suits your preferred coping style. Always choose approach rather than avoidance strategies, no matter your coping style.

Dealing with the demands of others

In your current situation, you will likely face numerous and repeated demands that make it more difficult to cope. These demands often relate to other people's needs rather than your own.

We are often unclear about our rights, particularly those related to our ability to take charge of our lives. Let's look at some of our mistaken assumptions that may relate to your current situation and your legitimate rights. We will also consider how holding these mistaken assumptions might affect how you react following the death of your loved one and how abandoning the mistaken assumption may improve your situation.

Table 4: Mistaken assumptions, their consequences and your legitimate rights.

Mistaken assumption	*It is selfish to put your needs before the needs of others.*
Consequence	You may end up not receiving the help and support you need to deal with your sense of loss and emotional pain. This is because you may not ask for help and support if other people are suffering or if you think others are too busy with their own lives.
Legitimate right	You have a right to put yourself first some of the time.
Outcome	Understanding this right may allow you to ask for the help and support your needs at this difficult time. The extent to which a person can offer you help and support should be determined by them, not by you.
Mistaken assumption	*You shouldn't take up other's valuable time with your own problems.*
Consequence	No one knows you need help because you did not say so. As a consequence, you do not receive the help you need.
Legitimate right	You have a right to ask for help or emotional support.
Outcome	The people who care about you will understand you need help, and they can offer you help if they can.
Mistaken assumption	*People don't want to hear you feel bad, so keep it to yourself.*

Consequence	Your feelings are never expressed, and you end up feeling bottled up and isolated.
Legitimate right	You have a right to feel and express pain.
Outcome	You will be able to feel some relief by sharing how you feel. Your emotional pain is not harmful to others who care about you. Friendships should be equal and reciprocal in that you should support your friends, and they should support you in times of distress. Accepting that people may be concerned about you frees you to express how you are feeling and allows your friends to do something for you at a time when it probably seems to them there is little they can do to make things better.
Mistaken assumption	*When someone takes the time to give you advice, you should take it seriously.*
Consequence	You may be overwhelmed by people telling you what to do. Unfortunately, the advice of one person can conflict with the advice of another, which only increases your confusion.
Legitimate right	You have a right to ignore the advice of others.
Outcome	You will come to realise that the advice people give you is only their opinion, and the final decision is yours to make. You should not then feel pressured to do what others demand or expect, especially if it contradicts what you need.
Mistaken assumption	*You should always try to accommodate others. If you don't, they won't be there when you need them.*
Consequence	You will be so busy thinking about what others need that you will have no opportunity to consider your own needs.
Legitimate right	You have a right to say no.
Outcome	You are the only person who truly knows how you are feeling, so you need to decide what you can take on and what you cannot. By understanding that you have the right to say no, you can pay attention to your own needs when they are greater than the needs of others.

Mistaken assumption	*Don't be anti-social. People are going to think you don't like them if you say you'd rather be alone instead of with them.*
Consequence	You will have no opportunity to have time by yourself to reflect on what has happened and how you are feeling if you give in to the demands of others to do what they are offering, such as thinking they are being helpful by ensuring people are around you all the time.
Legitimate right	You have a right to be alone, even if others would prefer your company.
Outcome	By understanding you have a right to time to yourself, you may be able to strike a good balance between being around others and being alone to deal with your thoughts and feelings
Mistaken assumption	*You should have a good reason for what you feel and do.*
Consequence	You waste energy thinking about how you present yourself to others and worrying about what they think about you.
Legitimate right	You have a right not to have to justify yourself to others.
Outcome	Particularly at times of intense distress, you should be able to express yourself without having to explain yourself to others who may have chosen to do things differently if they were in your situation.
Mistaken assumption	*When someone is in trouble, you should help them.*
Consequence	This may cause you to ignore your own needs in favour of the needs of others. This can result in your needs never being met.
Legitimate right	You have a right not to take responsibility for someone else's problem
Outcome	There are times in life when your needs exceed the needs of others, even if they are facing problems of their own. Understanding this may free you to focus on your own emotional reactions without worrying about the emotional reactions of others.

Mistaken assumption	*It is not nice to put people off. If questioned, give an answer.*
Consequence	Believing this, you may feel pressured to discuss things you do not want to discuss at times when you feel unable to discuss them.
Legitimate right	You have a right to choose not to respond to a situation.
Outcome	Curiosity on the part of the questioner does not give them the right to know or you an obligation to respond to their questioning. You are the person who decides what you disclose and when you disclose it. By accepting this, you can maintain your privacy if that is what you choose.

In many cases, asserting your legitimate rights is largely a matter of you accepting that these rights are legitimate and then calmly acting on that understanding. However, in other cases, you will be required to respond to a demand from someone else. You can adopt a straightforward strategy to doing this. It requires three simple steps.

Defining the problem as you see it.

Giving an account of how you feel about the problem.

Making a statement of what is going to occur or making a request for change.

Let's see how this works using the example of someone being intrusive in their curiosity about the circumstances of your loved one's death.

Defining the problem

"I understand you are interested in the details of what happened to my brother. You have been asking questions about what occurred."

Telling them how you feel

"I feel quite distressed when I am asked these types of questions because I am not yet able to talk about it."

Making a statement/request

"I am asking you to respect my need not to talk about it at the moment. I hope you understand."

You can say such things calmly and politely. In this way, you are asserting your rights without doing so aggressively or without passively abandoning your rights. Some people might keep pushing, but this requires only that you calmly repeat what you have already said. Remember, what you disclose and when you share information is up to you.

The same strategy can be applied in numerous situations where you feel under pressure. Remember, the goal is to assert your rights as you understand them. You are not being unreasonable by doing so.

Some final points

Some final points should be made or restated.

Recovery does not occur in a straight line. That is, you do not experience steady improvement, day after day, as time goes by. It would be nice if it did work this way because then you could predict the day when you would start to feel better. Rather than this straight trajectory, you can expect to experience ups and downs with how you are feeling. You will have some good days and some bad days.

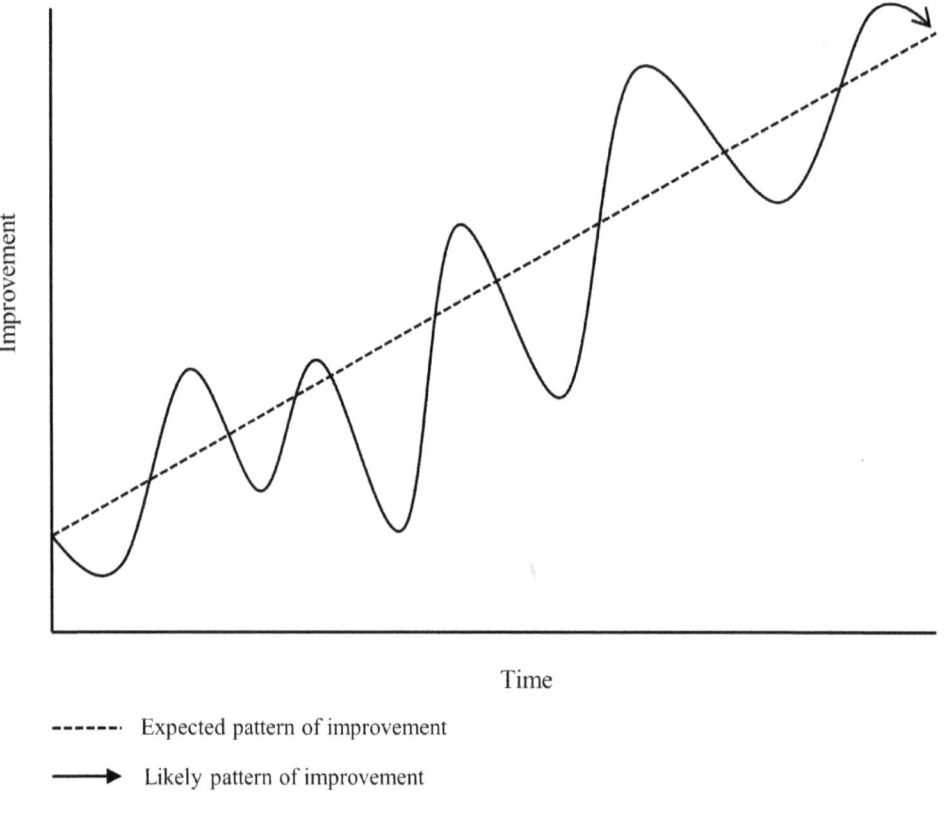

Figure 2: A depiction of the trajectory of recovery.

There will be difficult days as you experience any number of 'firsts'. These include the first time you go to do something that would typically involve the person who died, the first time you have a family gathering or a gathering of friends with the person you loved being absent, the first time your loved one is not there to support you through a situation when they would typically have done so. Anniversaries also will likely be difficult days. The anniversary of your loved one's death, birthdays, and other celebrations are all likely to present challenges for you. Expect these difficult days and aim to look after yourself when they occur. Understand these difficult days as a sign of the importance of your loved one to you.

There are many things in life that we experience that fall into the category of *'the way of things'*. By this, we mean that many things occur frequently enough to be considered somewhat common experiences in this world. Although we tend to think this way about positive experiences (e.g., childbirth) and some more negative experiences (e.g., death in old age), this notion can also be applied to other negative experiences. For example, we accept childbirth as the normal way of things and other events such as stillbirth and miscarriage are often thought about in the same way. The important point here is that it is a fact of life that people suicide. Therefore, there is no need for feelings like shame or guilt. Choose less complicated emotions to experience, like sadness or compassion.

Please understand that a person's decision to end their life does not define all of their life or determine who they were as an individual. There are many things about your loved one that you know to be true quite apart from how their life ended. Allow yourself to focus on those things.

We wish you well in coping with your loss.

Additional reading

Devine, M. (2018). *It's OK that you're not OK: Meeting grief and loss in a culture that doesn't understand.* Australia: St Martins Press.

Kubler-Ross, E., & Kessler, D. (2014). *On grief and grieving: Finding the meaning of grief through the five stages of loss.* US: Scribner Books.

Leenaars, A.A. (1991) (Ed.) *Life span perspectives of suicide: Time-lines in the suicide process.* US: Springer Nature.

Tobin, D., Holyrod, K., Reynolds, R., & Wigal, J.K. (1989). The hierarchical structure of the Coping Strategies Inventory. *Cognitive Therapy and Research, 13(4),* 343-361.

Worden, J.W. (2018). *Grief counseling and grief therapy: A handbook for the mental health practitioner (5th edn.).* US: Springer Publishing.

www.ingramcontent.com/pod-product-compliance
Lightning Source LLC
Chambersburg PA
CBHW080857090426
42735CB00014B/3173